KATHLYN GAY   MARTIN GAY

Twenty-First Century Books
Brookfield, Connecticut

Twenty-First Century Books
A Division of The Millbrook Press
2 Old New Milford Road
Brookfield, CT 06804

Library of Congress Cataloging-in-Publication Data
Gay, Kathlyn.
World War II / Kathlyn Gay and Martin Gay. — 1st ed.
p. cm. — (Voices from the past)
Includes bibliographical references and index.
1. World War, 1939–1945—Juvenile literature. [1. World War, 1939–1945.]
I. Gay, Martin, 1950– . II. Title. III. Series: Gay, Kathlyn. Voices from the past.
D743.7.G38 1995   95–12301
940.53—dc20   CIP
                                                                          AC
ISBN 0–8050–2849–8

Printed in the United States of America

10 9 8 7 6

Maps by Vantage Art, Inc.
Cover design by Karen Quigley
Interior design by Kelly Soong

Cover: "*. . . Manila Would Do*" by Keith Rocco
Courtesy of National Guard Heritage Series, Dept. of the Army,
National Guard Bureau, Washington, D.C.

Photo credits

pp. 8, 14, 28: The Bettmann Archive; pp. 10, 18, 21, 25, 31, 35, 36, 37, 50, 53, 56, 57:
UPI/Bettmann; pp. 29, 43: U.S. Center for Military History; pp. 44, 48: The Patton
Museum of Cavalry and Armor; p. 54: U.S. Marine Corps.

Contents

Acknowledgments

Some of the research for this series depended upon the special efforts of Dean Hamilton, who spent many hours locating primary source materials and other references on America's wars and sorting out appropriate stories among the many personal accounts available. Especially helpful was his work at the archival library of the University of South Florida at Tampa, researching for Spanish-American War and Civil War narratives. For the *World War I* title in this series, Dean also applied his special talents interviewing several of the few remaining veterans of WW I, obtaining their highly personal recollections, which the veterans allowed us to include. Thanks, Dean.

In addition, we would like to thank Lt. Col. (retired) John McGarrahan for locating narratives about personal experiences in the War of 1812, available in the archives at the Lilly Library, Indiana University, Bloomington, Indiana. We also thank Douglas Gay for obtaining narratives on the battle of Tippecanoe at the Tippecanoe County Historical Association in Lafayette, Indiana. Portions of these accounts are included in the *War of 1812* title in this series.

—*Kathlyn Gay and Martin Gay*

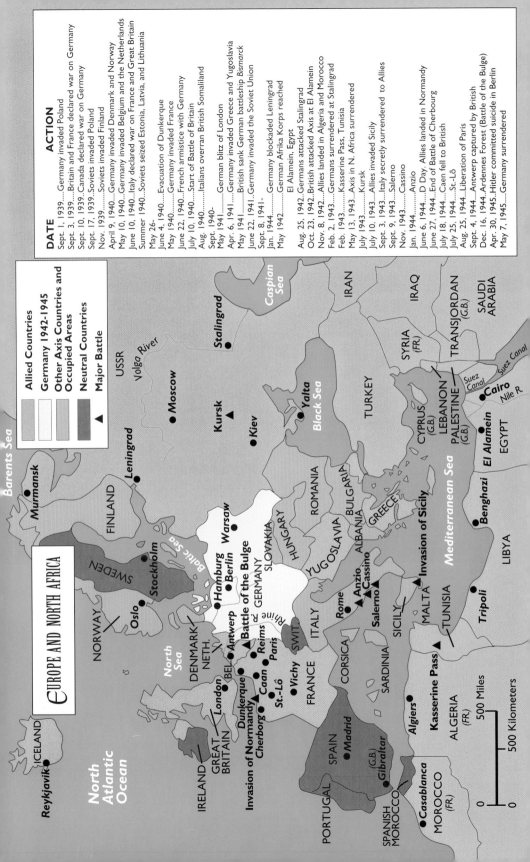

ASIA AND THE PACIFIC

Legend

- Allied areas
- Japan and Korea
- Areas held by Japan at the end of Aug. 1945
- Neutral Countries
- ▲ Major Battle

Date	Action
Dec. 7, 1941	Japanese attacked Pearl Harbor
Dec. 8, 1941	U.S., Canada, and Britain declared war on Japan
Dec. 8, 1941	Japanese attacked Hong Kong, Guam, and Wake; invaded Thailand
Dec. 9, 1941	China declared war on the Axis
Dec. 11, 1941	Germany and Italy declared war on the U.S.
Feb. 15, 1942	Singapore surrendered to Japanese

Feb. 26-28, 1942	Java Sea
Apr. 9, 1942	U.S. and Philippine troops on Bataan surrendered
Apr. 18, 1942	Doolittle's air raid on Tokyo
May 1942	The Coral Sea
June 4-6, 1942	Midway
summer 1942-mid 1944	New Guinea
Aug. 7, 1942-Feb. 1943	Guadalcanal
Nov. 1943	U.S. invaded Tarawa
Jan.-Feb. 1944	Kwajalein
Feb. 1944	Enewetak
Mar. 1944	Bougainville
June 19-20, 1944	Philippine Sea
June 1944	Saipan and Tinian
July-Aug. 1944	Guam
Sept. 1944	Peleliu
Oct. 20, 1944	Allies landed in the Philippines
Oct. 23-26, 1944	Leyte Gulf
Feb. 19-Mar. 16, 1945	Iwo Jima
May 1945	Rangoon fell to Allies
Apr. 1-June 21, 1945	Okinawa
Aug. 6, 1945	A-bomb dropped on Hiroshima
Aug. 8, 1945	Soviet Union declared war on Japan
Aug. 9, 1945	A bomb dropped on Nagasaki
Aug. 14, 1945	Japan surrendered

USSR

CANADA

ALASKA (U.S.)

TIBET

INDIA

Kohima

Imphal

BURMA

Rangoon

Ledo Road

Burma Road

CHINA

Chongqing

Beijing

MONGOLIA

MANCHURIA

Shanghai

Nagasaki

Hiroshima

Tokyo

KOREA

JAPAN

Taiwan

Hong Kong

THAILAND

INDOCHINA

MALAYA

Singapore

SUMATRA

BRUNEI

BORNEO

JAVA

South China Sea

Java Sea

Bataan

Luzon

Manila

Mindoro

PHILIPPINES

Leyte Gulf

Philippine Sea

Peleliu

Okinawa

Iwo Jima

Mariana Islands

Saipan

Tinian

Guam

Enewetak

Kwajalein

Caroline Islands

Truk Island

Marshall Islands

Tarawa

Gilbert Islands

Equator

Rabaul

NEW GUINEA

Bougainville

Guadalcanal

Coral Sea

Fiji Is.

AUSTRALIA

Darwin

Indian Ocean

Pacific Ocean

Bering Sea

Aleutian Islands

Attu Is.

Midway Island

Wake Island

Hawaiian Islands

Pearl Harbor

0   1000 Miles

0   1000 Kilometers

One

SNEAK ATTACK

December 7, 1941, was just another beautiful day in Hawaii, and a great one for flying. So that is what seventeen-year-old Roy Viousek and his father were doing, cruising in their small plane just after sunrise above the tranquil island paradise. The two flyers over Hawaii had the best seats in the house when a sneak attack by the Japanese Imperial Navy began, catapulting the United States into World War II. A witness to the events of that "date which will live in infamy," as President Franklin D. Roosevelt of the United States called it, reported that Roy and his father

> were two thousand feet over Oahu, able to see the first Japanese bomb explode in a Ford Island hangar. Roy thought it was a hangar fire and a flight of American P-40s. But as they dove to take a closer look, his father shouted, "P-40s, hell, they're Japs!" Afraid to land, they circled above the attacking planes for thirty minutes, hanging like bats over the attack, seeing bombs flash like mirrors as they caught the sun, then exploding in flashes and flame and sending waterspouts bursting skyward.[1]

In late November, the Japanese government secretly ordered a surprise attack on the U.S. Pacific Fleet, stationed

This aerial view was taken just as the attack on Pearl Harbor began. Torpedo tracks from Japanese minisubs are clearly visible.

at Pearl Harbor in the Hawaiian Islands, a U.S. territory. A Japanese task force maintained radio silence during negotiations with the United States while moving six aircraft carriers, two battleships, and several other warships and submarines into position. At 7:50 A.M. on December 7, wave after wave of heavily armed bombers and fast fighter planes—an attacking force of 360 planes—began dropping their lethal loads on Battleship Row. More than seventy-five U.S. ships were docked there, totally unaware that the Japanese were anywhere in the vicinity. Certainly they did not expect a sneak air raid.

SHOCK AND DEVASTATION

Months before the surprise attack, the U.S. government had cut off shipments of scrap metal, oil, and other materials to Japan, hoping to stem Japan's brutal aggression and conquests of land in Asia. Although the U.S. Pacific Fleet had received warnings that such actions might prompt a war with Japan, many Americans stationed at Pearl Harbor hoped that negotiations would prevent warfare. So when the attack came, some Americans in Hawaii were convinced that the first explosions were accidents or acts of God.

Lieutenant Colonel Herbert Blackwell was stationed at Fort Shafter in Hawaii at the time, and in a letter to his wife he related his surprise that this event even took place:

> When I got outside I was perfectly dumbfounded. Black columns of smoke were rising from Pearl Harbor Navy Yard, about three miles distant and the sky was filled with puffs of black smoke from AA shells. It looked like war, but I just could not believe my eyes. I just could not believe that Japan could make an air attack from such a distance without our Navy having some warning. The attack caught both the Army and Navy completely by surprise. Being Sunday morning most everyone was still in bed.[2]

That was the case for John Garcia, a sixteen-year-old apprentice pipe fitter who worked at Pearl Harbor in 1941. He recalled that his grandmother woke him at about 8:00 A.M. on December 7 to tell him that the Japanese had bombed Pearl Harbor and that a radio announcer had requested all harbor workers to report to work:

> I got out on my motorcycle and it took me five, ten minutes to get there. It was a mess.

I was working on the *U.S.S. Shaw*. It was on a floating dry dock. It was in flames. I started to go down into the pipe fitter's shop to get my toolbox when another wave of Japanese came in. I got under a set of concrete steps at the drydock where the battleship *Pennsylvania* was. An officer came by and asked me to go into the *Pennsylvania* and try to get the fires out. A bomb had penetrated the marine deck, and that was three decks below. Under that was the magazines: ammunition, powder, shells. I said, "There ain't no way I'm gonna go down there." It could blow up any minute. I was young and sixteen, not stupid, not at sixty-two cents an hour.[3]

In the United States, people also experienced shock and disbelief, which quickly turned to fear and panic. There were rumors that the Japanese would soon send a fleet of midget submarines to attack off U.S. shores. Dennis Keegan, like many other Americans living on the West Coast of the

Dense smoke and flames shoot from the USS West Virginia *and the USS* Tennessee *after the attack on Pearl Harbor.*

United States, planned to be ready. Keegan, a Californian, was sixteen years old and, as he described himself:

> a yell leader and C student at high school and very small. Because the Japanese were small, I thought I was their match. On Monday, December 8, about six of us were in a '36 Model A Ford, three in the front, three in the rumble seat, heading for Bodega Bay with our armament. Paul Henderson, a senior, had a .22. I had a .410. Scotty Webb had a little shotgun. Somebody else had a BB gun. We loaded our guns, hid behind the dunes, and waited for the Japanese assault.[4]

Although the feared Japanese attack on the continental United States did not happen, the almost undefended barrage on Hawaii lasted for just over two hours and resulted in more than 2,400 American deaths, 1,300 wounded, and another 1,000 missing. Eighteen ships sustained major damage. In addition, nearly 200 airplanes were destroyed or heavily damaged. By a fortunate happenstance, none of the U.S. aircraft carriers were docked at Pearl Harbor that day.

Japanese casualties numbered less than 100, and in all, twenty-nine of their planes and five of their submarines were destroyed. The Japanese tactical victory was thorough, but the Japanese miscalculation about the U.S. response was fatal to their long-term plans for domination of the Pacific. Apparently, they believed that the Americans would not have the will to fight a long war and would make peace in short order. But under the leadership of President Roosevelt, the country put all its industrial might and moral resolve into seeing that Japan, Germany, Italy, and the other nations that formed what was called the Axis powers were punished for their aggressions.

A CHANGE IN THE NEUTRAL POLICY

Up until the Pearl Harbor attack, the policy of the United States had been to maintain a neutral position and not get involved in the war going on in Europe. The war had begun on September 1, 1939, with a blitzkrieg, or lightning war, against Poland. This new type of warfare had been carefully planned by Adolf Hitler, ruthless head of the Nazi Party and German dictator. Without provocation, Hitler sent thousands of fighter planes and bombers, numerous fast-moving tanks, and ground troops in a simultaneous massive attack against Polish industrial plants, military installations, and troops. On September 17, the Union of Soviet Socialist Republics (USSR), which earlier had signed a Nazi-Soviet pact to intervene in a war with Poland, attacked from the east. Although Polish forces made valiant counterattacks, the country was soon overcome. The capital fell by the end of the month, and the Germans and Soviets divided Poland between them.

In August, before the German attack, France and Great Britain had formed an alliance with Poland to oppose any aggression, and thus they were drawn into the conflict. On September 3, they declared war on Germany. A week later, even though some Canadians believed their nation should remain neutral, Canada decided to support Great Britain and also declared war on Germany.

American citizens supported the policy of "isolationism." They felt that their distance from Europe, across the vast Atlantic Ocean, isolated them from the troubles that European countries were experiencing. These were severe troubles. Hitler's troops had quickly overrun not only Poland but also Norway, Luxembourg, Belgium, and the Netherlands. By June of 1940, Italy had entered the war on the side of the Germans, and the seemingly invincible French army had surrendered its country to a puppet government installed by the German Nazis.

President Roosevelt feared that the United States would become more and more vulnerable as the German advance continued, so he asked the federal government to authorize the buildup of American military forces. By the time of the Pearl Harbor attack, the United States was spending $2 billion per month on war supplies. A large portion of the money was used in a program called Lend-Lease—the federal government loaned funds or bought war equipment and food that was sent to nations thought to be vital to the defense of the United States. Through the program, aid went first to Great Britain and later to the USSR, which had joined the Allies after being attacked by the Nazis in June 1941.

BATTLE OF BRITAIN

Although sentiment to remain out of the fray remained strong in most parts of the country during 1940 and most of 1941, many Americans anxiously followed Hitler's progress. In 1940, Hitler turned his full attention to the invasion of Great Britain. Germany planned to send in planes to bomb the Royal Air Force (RAF) and Royal Navy installations in the southern part of England in order to soften the defenses against a full military invasion. German pilots flew more than 2,000 fighters and bombers in daily missions against some 600 British fighters. It seemed that the plucky but far outnumbered forces of the RAF would eventually lose. Indeed, by September 5, 1940, only 200 British planes remained.

Then the RAF took the offensive and began bombing runs against Berlin, the capital of Germany. Hitler, in response, redirected the Luftwaffe (German air force) to concentrate bombing on England's capital, London. Night after night, the bombers dropped their loads on the city, which had to learn to live in total blackout so the German pilots would not have any landmarks to aid their targeting.

Horace Basham was a young man during that time, and he recalled how the bombing affected him his entire life:

> At the time of the so called Battle of Britain I was not yet 19 years of age. I then lived with my parents brothers and sister in Plaistow in West Ham. . . . I experienced the intensive bombing of London just as millions of other Londoners. Even today I start when ever a loud bang of noise comes unexpectedly.[5]

The German air force bombed London night after night and caused great damage to the city.

The blitz of English cities, known as the Battle of Britain, was designed to force Britain's surrender before the United States could come to its aid. Air attacks continued until May of 1941, but the British, under the leadership of their prime minister, Winston Churchill, held fast. England suffered terrible losses of life and much destruction, but for the first time German forces were stopped in Europe. As Churchill noted in an address to his people citing the bravery and skill of the RAF pilots, "Never, in the field of human conflict, was so much owed by so many to so few."

Although the Germans were not able to defeat the British, they made good progress in their execution of the war. They had long planned to abandon the Nazi-Soviet pact and invade the Soviet Union to establish German colonies and provide more *Lebensraum,* or living space, for the German people. On June 22, 1941, Germany assaulted the Soviet territories in eastern Europe. The last thing the Nazis needed was for the United States to enter on the side of the Allies, which eventually included the four major powers— Great Britain, the USSR, China, and the United States—and forty-six other nations. The Allies fought the Axis powers of Germany, Italy, and Japan, plus six other nations. Japan, like Germany, had definite plans to counter the Allied threat.

Two

JAPANESE ADVANCES

Certainly the surprise attack on Pearl Harbor was a critical part of the Japanese plan. By striking fast and in secret while negotiations were taking place, the imperial government of Emperor Hirohito and his war minister, General Tojo Hideki, saw an opportunity to eliminate the potential threat of U.S. resistance.

Prior to the attack on the U.S. fleet, Japan had pursued a course of territorial expansion for a decade, gaining large chunks of land from its neighbors in the Far East. Japan's invasion of Manchuria in 1931 started the expansion process, and in 1937 the Japanese made a successful full-scale assault against China. By 1940, they controlled the eastern part of that most populous nation, and they were soon marching into southern Indochina.

That same year, Japan and Germany signed a pact creating the Greater East Asia Coprosperity Sphere. This pact was merely an excuse for them to dominate all of the countries located in that part of the world.

This worrisome state of affairs finally caused the U.S. government to take diplomatic action. President Roosevelt banned U.S. exports to Japan and froze all Japanese assets in the United States.

In Japan, military leaders continued a major antiforeign campaign that had been going on since the assault against China. In the view of Alice-Leone Moats, a U.S. news correspondent in Tokyo, the "most violent manifestation" of the campaign was "the spy phobias which possessed all inhabitants of Nippon [Japan]. . . . No one believed that a foreigner could possibly be living in or visiting Japan for any simple reason such as business or pleasure. He must be in the pay of a foreign government—any government. This entailed a counterespionage system."

According to Moats, "It was a crime to take pictures from any height above twenty yards." Posters were also displayed "in all cities and towns warning the inhabitants against foreign agents." Foreigners living in Japan were suspect if they had too much contact with their own embassy. Japanese servants of foreigners were required to report on all activities of their employers. Through these and other methods, the military leaders were able to develop "a strong feeling of hatred for all Westerners" among many of the Japanese people.[1]

By September 1941, General Tojo was convinced that the United States meant to strangle his country by depriving it of critical raw materials. He was certain war with America was inevitable and that it would be better to attack first and gain the advantage. More moderate Japanese leaders wanted to continue negotiating with the Americans in an attempt to ease the sanctions and keep the United States neutral as long as possible.

After making no progress in his efforts to resolve differences with the U.S. peacefully, the civilian prime minister of Japan stepped down in mid-October 1941. Tojo took his

Cordell Hull (center) escorts Japan's special envoy Saburo Kurusu (right) and Japanese ambassador Kichisaburo Nomura (left) to a meeting with President Roosevelt on November 17, 1941. By then, the plan to attack Pearl Harbor was already in place.

place and established a war cabinet of advisers. Talks between U.S. secretary of state Cordell Hull and Japanese emissaries continued, but the two sides remained far apart.

Because Americans had broken the Japanese code used to transmit instructions to the negotiating team, U.S. officials knew that rejection of the Japanese demands to end the embargo would likely lead to war. Nevertheless, on November 26, Secretary Hull formally restated the U.S. position: Japan must withdraw from China and Indochina and end territorial expansion. The die was cast, and the Japanese fleet soon disembarked for Hawaii.

CONCURRENT ATTACKS

About the same time that the Japanese attacked Hawaii, they also began a series of attacks on U.S. islands in the western Pacific and portions of southeastern Asia. Within days they captured Wake Island, Guam, Hong Kong, and Singapore, then moved on toward the Philippines. The United States had sent General Douglas MacArthur to defend U.S. territory in the Pacific, particularly the Philippine Islands, which were critical because of their close proximity to Japan. MacArthur commanded 55,000 Filipinos and Americans when the Japanese began to land troops, launching massive air and sea forces against Luzon, the main island in the Philippines.

MacArthur's troops were forced to retreat to the Bataan Peninsula. Many American and Filipino soldiers were captured by the Japanese, who marched their captives 80 miles (130 kilometers) through dense, hot jungles to prison camps. There was little food or clean water, and some soldiers were driven insane by thirst or died after drinking from bacteria-laden streams or wells. And there was always the threat of beatings or being shot by guards if a soldier dropped from exhaustion and illness. Homer Boren, one survivor of this Bataan Death March, as it became known, recorded how he longed to die but still fought to survive.

On the march, Boren saw dead and dying prisoners all along the way. "One prisoner lying beside the road made an especially vivid impression on me," Boren recounted years later. "He was more dead than alive, and his complexion had turned dark, as if he had the Black Plague. Green flies crawled in and out of his nostrils and open mouth, and he was covered with gaping, infected sores. Seeing that he was too weak to even sweep the flies from his face, guards had left him alone to die a slow, agonizing death."[2]

The U.S. forces retreated even farther to Corregidor, an island in the middle of Manila Bay, where they faced inevitable defeat. As one U.S. radioman reported in his last Morse code transmission on May 6, 1942:

We've got about 55 minutes now and I feel sick at my stomach. I am really low down. . . . Just made broadcast to Manila

to arrange surrender. . . . I can hardly think. Can't think at all.
. . . The jig is up. Everyone is bawling like a baby. They are pil-
ing dead and wounded in our tunnel. . . . I know now how a
mouse feels. Caught in a trap waiting for guys to come
along and finish it. Got a treat. Can pineapple. Opening it
with a Signal Corp knife. . . . My name is Irving Stobing. Get
this to my mother.[3]

MORE JAPANESE VICTORIES

Japanese forces also moved into southern Burma from
Thailand. The British, who were in possession of that
ground, were driven back to the capital, Rangoon.
Meanwhile, the Chinese government under Chiang Kai-shek
attempted to bolster the Allied position in Burma. In March
1942, an American general, Joseph W. Stilwell, became
General Chiang Kai-shek's army chief of staff. He commanded the Fifth and Sixth Chinese Armies in Burma.

Cut off by the Japanese in April, Stilwell's forces covered the British retreat into India and were almost defeated
themselves. They had to fight long and hard to make it back
to China.

Assisting in this effort was American general Claire L.
Chennault and the Flying Tigers, a group of American volunteer pilots who had set up an air base near Rangoon.
Colonel Robert L. Scott flew a P-40 with the distinctive deco-
rations of the Flying Tigers: the planes were painted in the
front to represent the gaping mouth and sinister eyes of a
wild and hungry shark. His recollection of a first encounter
with the enemy illustrates the attitude of these volunteers:

Keeping very low again, I turned East and found the Burma
Road, turned up it and started looking for the columns
which I knew were Japanese. I approached them from the

American pilots at a base in China race toward their P-40s.

rear, fired from a thousand yards, and the road seemed to pulverize. The closely packed troops appeared to rush back towards me as my speed cut the distance between us. I held the six guns on as I went the length of the troop column and caught the trucks.... Straight back to the base I went, feeling very intoxicated with success.... [The Japanese] had been treated just as they had been treating Allied ground troops, and I was happy.[4]

The flying corps stayed in Burma until July 4, 1942, harassing the Japanese. Even though the Flying Tigers downed 297 Japanese planes and killed about 500 of the enemy, they could not halt the Japanese offensive.

JAPANESE GAINS IN THE PACIFIC

In 1942, the Japanese advance throughout Southeast Asia seemed unstoppable, and the United States and the Allied forces were at a low point. Americans were uniformly behind the war effort, but they still needed a victory to bolster their morale. Lieutenant Colonel James H. Doolittle of the U.S. Army Air Corps knew how important it was to show that the Japanese were not invincible.

On April 18, Doolittle initiated an attack, leading a squadron of B-25 bombers that took off from an aircraft carrier in the Pacific Ocean. He led his planes very low over the Japanese Islands and dropped the first bombs on Tokyo. Although the bombing raid had almost no strategic military importance, psychologically it was a tremendous first victory for Americans.

Yet, the U.S. government had already decided that the main thrust of its might would not be against Japan at this time. Germany was considered much more dangerous. Germans had advanced along the Russian front and were expected to soon launch a land invasion of England, which meant that those Allies must be protected. The United States also agreed with Winston Churchill that "the defeat of Germany, entailing a collapse, will leave Japan exposed to overwhelming force, whereas the defeat of Japan would not by any means bring the World War to an end."[5]

Three

✦

GREAT CHANGES AT HOME

$\mathcal{T}$wo years before the attack on Pearl Harbor, President Roosevelt and others in the federal government had made certain that the production of war supplies was a top priority. But the administration soon realized that to fight this war all over the world they had to spur an unprecedented industrial response. All key U.S. industries, often called "defense factories," began working twenty-four hours every day of the week. By December 1942, a year after Pearl Harbor, the U.S. output of military equipment and other war goods equaled that of all Axis nations combined.

Mobilization for war brought about many changes in daily life. Rationing was needed to conserve items in short supply, especially those that had to be imported, such as sugar and rubber. Vast migrations of people from rural areas to cities took place. Hundreds of thousands of black Americans left the South and moved to the North for good-paying jobs in war factories. Some white workers resented the competition for jobs as well as for the limited housing available and protested, creating racial tensions and riots in some northern cities. But for the first time, a U.S. president issued an executive order outlawing discriminatory hiring in defense factories and in the federal government, although that certainly did not end discrimination throughout the United States.

There was also great social upheaval when families moved or were separated because of military duties. Some devastating changes were forced on families of Japanese ancestry, who were loyal American citizens but were labeled "a menace" and a threat to national security—in both the United States and Canada.

RETALIATION AGAINST PEOPLE OF JAPANESE HERITAGE

Even though Japanese immigrants and their families had lived peacefully for several generations as farmers, business-people, and small shop owners in the United States, prejudice against them had been strong prior to the war. With the attack on Pearl Harbor, the hatemongers were easily able to sway public opinion, convincing many Americans that people of Japanese descent were suspect. U.S. military leaders believed that Americans with ties to Japan would turn against the United States and would sabotage the many military installations along the West Coast, where most people of Japanese heritage lived.

There had been no acts of disloyalty among Japanese Americans, but they were constantly under surveillance. U.S. citizens of German and Italian heritage also were victims of discrimination, but for the most part they were not considered national security risks, even though Germany and Italy were Axis nations.

In February 1942, military officials convinced President Roosevelt and the Justice Department to authorize the relocation of thousands of people of Japanese heritage—two-thirds of them American citizens—away from the coast to inland camps guarded by the U.S. military. Canada undertook similar measures, moving about 23,000 people of

Japanese heritage out of Canadian coastal areas in the west.

More than forty years later, the United States government tried to make amends for denying the liberties of 112,000 of its citizens. In 1987, the U.S. Congress issued a formal apology and passed a law authorizing a token payment of at least $20,000 to each of the more than 60,000 survivors of the internment camps.

Kiyo Sato, born in the United States of Japanese immigrant parents who were U.S. citizens, is one of those survivors. She explained what happened to her after the relocation order took effect:

> I walked in the house after school and knew in an instant that something ominous was happening. My mother was sitting in a chair, alone, hands folded in her lap. . . . She pointed

The relocation center at Heart Mountain, Colorado, had a central dining area for all the Japanese interned there for the duration of the war.

to my room. Through a half open door I could see a man with a hat sitting at my desk. He was reading what looked to me like my diary. My first reaction was to rush in and grab it away from him. . . . But Mama whispered that there was another man in the attic and still another somewhere outside. "FBI," she said, and my heart froze. . . . I was worried. Mr. Saiki, a family friend, had been whisked away last week. His crime: He had among his possessions a flashlight. An old battery was found in the shed of Mr. Okazaki, another friend. Neither was given time to pack anything, and no one knew exactly where they were taken. Some thought they might be in a concentration camp in Montana.[1]

In spite of the fact that one of Kiyo's brothers was serving in the U.S. Army, she and her family were forced to leave their California home, giving up their land and many personal possessions. Like others of Japanese descent, they were herded onto a train for transport to an unknown destination. "Two army boys with guns" guarded both sides of the train car that the Sato family rode in all through the night. By morning, the train had reached the end of the line and everyone was herded into open army trucks.

"We rode for miles into the sagebrush. Dust was everywhere; black hair turned brown, eyebrows and eyelashes drooped with the brown dust. We looked at each other and laughed, but soon the weariness and the pounding heat sagged our spirits," Kiyo reported. Eventually she and her family, along with hundreds of others, ended up on the Potson Indian Reservation in the desert, where they lived for months in "tarpapered barracks" that "stretched out as far as one could see." Families usually shared a single room in the barracks, and there was no indoor plumbing.

Similar "relocation centers" were set up in other remote areas of the United States. Barbed wire surrounded the camps, and armed guards watched over these American citizens until near the end of the war. In spite of this degrading and unjust treatment, many men from the camps volunteered to serve in the armed forces—in segregated units—and performed with distinction.

RECRUITMENT FOR THE MILITARY AND THE WORKPLACE

By the spring of 1942, there was a growing manpower shortage in the military. Posters, newspapers, magazines, radio, movies, and stage plays urged both men and women to sign up for military service. In American wars prior to World War II, there had been debate about and opposition to using women in the armed forces. Now, as men went off to battle, women were needed for noncombat jobs such as stenographers, mechanics, drivers, and switchboard operators.

During World War II, more than 100,000 women served in the Women's Army Auxiliary Corps (WAAC), which later became the Women's Army Corps (WAC). Some women signed up for the U.S. Marines and Coast Guard. Women also joined the U.S. Navy as WAVES (Women Accepted for Volunteer Emergency Service), shortened to WAVE. One WAVE of South Bend, Indiana, Mary Wishin, worked in naval communications for two years. "We were top secret guys. We broke the German code,"[2] she said, a feat that certainly helped the Allies win battles in the war.

In the fall of 1942, the Women's Auxiliary Air Squadron, later known as the Women's Air Force (WAF), began training women pilots who ferried planes to various military bases in the United States. They also tested aircraft and performed other noncombat flight duties.

One WAF summed up the feeling of many women in the armed forces at that time: "All of us realized what a spot we were in. We had to deliver the goods."[3] Many of the

Members of the Women's Air Force were trained as pilots to ferry aircraft.

women believed they might never again be allowed to serve in the military if they did not prove to be capable in their chosen roles.

Media propaganda also urged Americans—women primarily—to "Get a War Job." Before the war, most of the jobs in the factories were held by men, who were then considered the breadwinners and heads of the household. When some sixteen million males enlisted or were drafted into the military, however, employers heavily recruited women to fill the spots on the assembly lines of what were referred to as "essential industries." Opportunities for women also opened up in male-dominated fields such as science.

Many women began working outside the home for the first time. Norman Rockwell, a popular artist of the day, defined the ideal of the female worker when he painted *Rosie the Riveter* for a cover of the *Saturday Evening Post* magazine. But there was much substance behind that romantic image of a woman wearing cute overalls and a turban about her head.

Nell Giles was a staff writer for the *Boston Globe* when she took a job in a plant operated by General Electric. Her regular columns for the paper preserved some of the flavor of her experience as a "Rosie":

> I've just finished my first day on a factory bench and I honestly wonder how I can ever go back to the humdrum world of people who don't make the wheels that go round! I'm here for the summer, and the censor won't allow me to tell you where "here" is, but I can say that what we make is precision instruments for planes. Some of our instruments were on Jimmy Doolittle's dashboard that day over Tokyo.[4]

Across the Atlantic Ocean, similar war production work involved large numbers of women, but in Europe there was little choice. Women were expected, if not required, to do their part for the war effort. In England, for example, Anne Oliver was "called up" to aid in food production immediately

Many women worked in industry during the war. Here, a former waitress helps to construct the Liberty Ship SS George Washington Carver *in early 1943.*

after completing her studies at Liverpool University. She was assigned duty at a farm, where her day began at 6 A.M. At that hour in the winter, it was "still quite dark and often very cold." She recalled:

> I would go straight down to the farmyard to be told what jobs to start on, probably cleaning out pig-sties or stables by lantern-light. . . . Then out into the fields to feed the sheep. This meant harnessing a cart-horse . . . loading a cart with turnips and some sheep-fodder . . . [and leading] the horse up to the sheep-field with it. . . . After that—field work, hoeing sugar-beet perhaps—until dinner at one pm, then more work . . . until 5pm. Then feed the chickens and then off to my supper at 6pm.[5]

VOLUNTEERS AND WAR RATIONS

The war effort on the home front also depended on volunteer work. In many U.S. cities and towns, an Office of Civilian Defense trained volunteer workers to defend their communities in case there was an enemy air attack. Civil defense workers conducted air raid drills, practiced disaster and rescue operations, and learned how to control traffic and crowds in a panic. Emergency Food and Housing Corps volunteers prepared to provide food and shelter for people left homeless after an air raid. Many people answered the call to "Volunteer for Victory. Offer *your* service to *your* RED CROSS," as one poster put it.

Even if a person did not directly contribute to the cause, every citizen was affected by the shortage of some consumer goods. Some factories that once manufactured bicycles or toys, for instance, were retooled to make bombs and rifles. People saved waste fats to use in the manufacture of explosives. Children often collected newspapers for recycling and saved scrap metal and aluminum, which were sent to refineries, then reused to make war equipment.

Food was needed for the vast armies doing battle all over the globe. The federal government ordered shipments of foods high in protein and energy, such as meats and butter, sent to troops overseas. Preserved fruits and vegetables were also sent. Citizens planted "victory gardens" to supplement their own food supplies. Goods like sugar and meat could only be purchased, in limited quantities, with War Ration Stamps, which were issued to American citizens by the government.

The instructions with the original U.S. ration books were very clear: "Everyone must see that his War Ration Book is kept in a safe place and properly used. . . . When you buy any rationed product, the proper stamp must be detached in the presence of the storekeeper."[6]

Of course, no war could be fought and won without funds. The U.S. government issued billions of dollars' worth of bonds, stamps, and certificates that citizens bought to help pay for war goods. "Buy war bonds!" was a common slo-

A group of Hollywood stars open a bond drive in Washington, D.C., on August 31, 1942.

gan. People could later cash in the bonds, earning interest for the time their money had been used by the government. Various taxes also helped raise money for the cost of the war, which eventually totaled about $300 billion for the United States. The overall cost worldwide was estimated at well over $1 trillion.

The greatest cost, however, was in human lives. No one knows how many people actually died in World War II, but the United States lost at least 292,000 military personnel and some 6,000 civilians—a relatively small number compared to the fifteen to twenty million killed in battle throughout the world.

Four

SACRIFICES

The shared sacrifices at this time were beyond any commitment made by Americans in any previous war. No one wanted to be involved in a world war, but most willingly did what they could to help. Nell Giles made this point in one of her columns about women working on the war assembly line. She explained that a young woman wanted

> to leave her secretarial position to join us on the work bench and help make precision instruments for planes. She is engaged to a young American who is wearing his wings in Australia. But, her mother protested, she is too young. . . .
>
> Surely there are millions of mothers in America today who feel the same way. Mine does. Neither are these mothers happy that their sons have left good jobs and their way of life to get up at dawn, drill, wash their own clothes, learn to shoot a machine gun and then say good-by for the duration of war or life.
>
> As the philosophers always say, the tragedy of war is that the old folks plan it and the young folks fight it. But young or old, you can't IGNORE the war. Business is NOT "as usual" and neither are you.[1]

Certainly business was not "as usual" for those who served in the military. Not long after the United States, Canada, and Great Britain declared war on Japan on December 8, 1941, the U.S. Congress passed a declaration of war against Germany and Italy. While American armed forces held off Japanese advances in the Pacific and Southeast Asia, they also assisted the Allies in North Africa and Europe.

Hitler kept up two fronts of the war after he broke off the attack on the British Isles. Italian reverses in North Africa forced him to send many men and arms there in order to solidify gains that had been made earlier. The British, under General Bernard Montgomery, were able to push these troops back to where they had been a year before. In this effort, Montgomery received substantial aid from the United States in the form of tanks and ammunition.

Montgomery's British army and newly deployed American forces under General Dwight D. Eisenhower faced Germany's crack desert troops led by the brilliant field marshall Erwin Rommel. The Allies claimed a major victory when they caught fifteen German divisions in a vicelike operation on May 12, 1943. The battle in North Africa gave the untried American fighters valuable war experience against the German soldiers. This lesson would prove critical as the Allies prepared to launch a counteroffensive to help the Russians put down the German invasion of their homeland.

There was some disagreement between the British and the Americans about how the war should proceed. U.S. generals called for a direct assault on Europe, preferably landing a massive wave of men and equipment in France. The English military, on the other hand, thought that it was best to follow Churchill's advice and "peck at the periphery."

After their success in North Africa, the Allies (with the

Allied tanks in spread-out formation go on the attack in Tunisia.
Rommel's Afrika Korps defeated the Americans in a hard-fought
battle near Kasserine Pass in February 1943.

Americans reluctantly agreeing) decided to move into
Europe from the Mediterranean. An assault on Italy was
planned. This was not what the Russians wanted. They needed more direct relief to fend off the German army, which was
all over the western part of their country.

THE RUSSIAN FRONT

Following the initial thrust in the summer of 1941, the
German advance in Russia began to slow. In the winter
months, after constant fighting, the Germans reached
Moscow, but the terrible freezing weather and a strong Allied
counteroffensive pushed German forces back 60 miles (100
kilometers) in short order.

By the next spring, the invaders were making little
progress. Supply lines were stretched too far, resistance was

stiff, and as Major Siegfried Knappe of the invading German army noted, occupying such a vast space was not simple:

> Every day of marching was just like every other day. It turned very hot in late summer, and the heat and insects did not go away at night. Nothing could have prepared us for the mental depression brought on by this realization of the utter physical vastness of Russia. Tiny little doubts began to creep into our minds. Was it even possible that such vast emptiness could be conquered by foot soldiers?

The major's recollection of that difficult time revealed more than doubts about spreading a poorly equipped army over far too vast a territory. He recognized what many who have experienced war have noted over and over again: there is common human suffering. As Knappe wrote:

> Sometimes during the fighting the Russians would shell their own villages if we were in them. When that happened, the

Russians would destroy their own villages rather than leave anything for the Germans.

Russian civilians were in the same boat we were in, and in situations like that, nationality is not a factor—survival is all that matters. We would all just try to protect ourselves, and we also protected the others if we could. They cooperated with us in extinguishing lights at night and keeping their windows covered. At times it became almost a conspiracy. I have a vivid recollection of lying on the ground near a peasant hut as Russian artillery shells exploded nearby. I slowly became aware of an elderly Russian peasant woman lying near me. When she saw me look at her, she smiled reassuringly. She reminded me of nothing so much as a mother reassuring her child.[2]

Fighting on the Russian front moved back and forth over a very long line, with great losses of life and limb. The Germans and their partners alone suffered over 800,000 casualties in this theater of the war. But there was always some doubt about whether the Russians would be able to hold back the continual German barrage.

The Russian fortress city of Sebastopol fell to the Germans after a siege of nine months. Here, Germans atop a light tank view the devastation.

In late 1942 and early 1943, the United States and England set a strategy to put more pressure on Germany's rear flank. By this time, America's production of bombers and bombs was in full swing, and the Allies decided to attack German cities and German-dominated areas with massive air strikes. For instance, a May 1942 RAF raid on Cologne devastated that city with 1,000-pound bombs. All over German-held land, the citizens suffered under the constant attacks.

One who experienced the bombings was Walter Felscher, who was thirteen years old at the time and lived in Brandenburg, about 40 miles (65 kilometers) west of Berlin, the capital of Germany. He described what it was like to be on the ground when the Allies came to bomb:

> On the average, there was an air alarm on five nights of the week. Usually at about 9:15 when the British bombers flew to Berlin and passed over our area—it lasted, say, until 11 pm. Maybe once per week there was a second air alarm at about 1 am, and I well remember my mother's efforts to get me out of bed and have myself dressed. Then everybody from the house's 7 apartments rushed down into the cellar where a room had been set up as *Luftschutzraum*, in a corner of two of the heavier foundation walls, all made of brick and mortar....
>
> The air alarms during the day occurred maybe twice a week.... I sneaked out of the Luftschutzraum and watched the sky.... There would begin a slow, distant hum, which would grow into a roar ... and then in the blue sky the tip of a very fat white pencil would appear, two fingers wide if you looked up, and slowly it would cross the sky from west to east: the white exhaust fumes of hundreds of planes, flying in tight formation towards Berlin.... No anti-aircraft guns

would fire—the planes were too high—no German planes anywhere that would have attacked the procession. He, who saw this perfect air power, could not believe in German victory anymore, unless he believed in miracles.

Although Brandenburg escaped the bombings during most of the war, the town was hit on the Saturday before Easter in 1945, when many people "were in town to do their Easter shopping." As Felscher recalled:

The air raid siren had hardly sounded when the first bombs fell, making the earth tremble. We barely made it to the cellar and sat shaking for the 10 minutes or so which it lasted. When we came up, our house had not been hit, but the waves of air pressure had heaved the big front doorway out of its angles and it lay splintered on its side. And most of the windows had been blown out.

It had been a bombing of the town, not of the factories, and hundreds of people were left dead. There were two kinds of bombs then: explosive ones, which would smash an entire building leaving a deep crater, and incendiary bombs ... which would just crash through the roof and set the house afire. Incendiary bombs ... could be extinguished with sand (no, not with water), and in most houses heaps of sand had been set up in the rooms under the roof, and two or three of the inhabitants would watch and, in case such bombs fell, would run up and try to extinguish them.

Such a fire guard, consisting of six or seven teachers, [had] been set up for our school, and while, of course, on Easter Saturday no school was held, those teachers had come to their guard duty before the alarm sounded. But it were not incendiary bombs which hit the school, it were explosives. The building collapsed into a huge heap of bricks, locking the teachers into the cellar. And the main water pipes passing through the cellars broke. They all drowned. And while a pupil . . . usually hasn't particular affections for his teachers: even to the mean ones I wouldn't have wished that kind of death.[3]

ENDING WAR IN EUROPE

$\mathcal{B}$ritish and American forces landed in Sicily at the start of the invasion of Italy on July 9 and 10, 1943. They hoped to follow up on the gains they had achieved in North Africa. At the beginning, the combined forces made great progress, but soon after, the Germans threw all their might into the defense of their positions.

Within a few months, however, the Allied invasion of the Italian Peninsula contributed to the fall of Mussolini, the Fascist leader who had sided with Hitler. The new Italian government reversed allegiances and declared war on Germany in October 1943; difficult Allied fighting against the Germans in mountainous areas continued in Italy until the end of the war.

D-DAY INVASION

With the Italian reversal, the way was clear for a massive invasion of France, which the American forces had called for since the beginning of their involvement. Almost three million Britains, Canadians, and Americans were assembled and thousands of ships and planes were readied for the invasion, which became known as D Day. Horace Basham was with the British Royal Air Force on that day.

Inducted into the Royal Air Force one day before his nineteenth birthday, Basham had served nearly four years as an aircraft mechanic in the south of England. He recalled the outset of the Normandy invasion and what he described as "the pre-softening up of the landing areas." He explained:

> You may have heard of the thousand bomber raids. At this time it seemed there were several thousand bombers in the sky.
>
> This particular morning very early a great noise was heard coming from inland, soon to be followed by masses of lights in the sky. Great masses of bombers, all with the navigation lights on, I don't believe this had ever been heard of in all the history of air warfare. But it was necessary to avoid mid air collisions. . . .To see and hear this great armada slowly crossing the sky was awesome to say the least. That was the beginning of D-Day. Masses of US bomber squadrons, and RAF Lancaster bombers towing gliders of paratroops: these heading for Holland to capture vital bridges and communications points.[1]

These operations were part of the most powerful invasion force ever assembled. For two months, troops and equipment had been brought to England in preparation for what was code-named Operation Overlord. General Dwight D. Eisenhower led the assault against continental Europe.

On June 6, 1944, some 4,000 ships left England's coast for the short trip across the English Channel to carry tens of thousands of troops in an amphibious invasion of the French coast. The initial assault was supported by 9,500 aircraft. By the third week of the invasion more than a million Allied troops were strung out along the French northwest coastline.

American forces land on the northern coast of France on
D Day, June 6, 1944. The 176,000 troops from the United States,
Canada, Britain, and France faced heavy resistance from the Germans.

Corporal William Preston served with a tank battalion, and he wrote to his father about the experience he had after the landing on the beach:

> In front of us were cliffs, and to the right there were two exits from our beach through the cliffs to higher ground. Both of these were mined and defended heavily. In the cliffs were a whole series of underground fortifications, mostly interconnecting machine gun nests. These played hell with our infantry and engineers as they came through the obstacles. Some never got through, some fell and were claimed by a rising tide, but others slowly worked their way past the high water mark to the base of the cliff. It took real guts for these boys to advance.[2]

Among the tank troops was the first armored black unit ever to fight with the U.S. Army, the 761st Tank Battalion. The men served at the request of General George Patton, who told them, "I would never have asked for you if you weren't good. I don't care what color you are so long as you go up there and kill those Kraut[s]."[3]

From the beginning of the U.S. involvement in World War II, all branches of the military were segregated, with separate units for whites and nonwhites. The U.S. War Department and most military leaders had adamantly refused to allow integration, and "the hypocrisy involved in setting up a

An M4 medium tank of the 761st Tank Battalion
heads into action in France in 1944.

segregated army to fight an enemy with a master-race ideology was apparent to all Black troops," declared one researcher of black history.[4]

Second-class status often made many black military men angry, but "it did not make them disloyal," wrote columnist Cynthia Tucker of the *Seattle Times*. In a 1994 editorial about her father and three uncles, who are World War II veterans, she pointed out that the men "are proud to have served their country, even though the World War II draft began during a time when the military hierarchy was still convinced that black men could not be trained to fight." One of her uncles joined the navy, and he "vividly recalled the day he was shipped off from Monroeville [Alabama]. Before the raw recruits boarded the bus, they were all given a meal at a local cafe. While the white recruits were fed inside, the black soldiers were fed off an automobile grease rack in a nearby service station, which was lowered to waist height to serve as a table."

Another uncle came back to the United States after two years in Europe and was stationed in Virginia. Tucker related that "he and a friend set out for a day trip into Washington, D.C., by civilian bus. Halfway there, the bus driver told them they would have to move to the back of the bus. They did not. 'We never exchanged a word with him. We just didn't move. We were not in a mood to be pushed around,' [her uncle] recalled."[5]

Although more than 1.2 million troops of African ancestry served in World War II, no black World War II soldier has yet received a Medal of Honor. Because of charges that racism played a role in choosing Medal of Honor recipients, the U.S. Army announced in April 1993 that it would reexamine recommendations made for black soldiers who might be eligible for the award.

After American troops landed in the south of France, progress was quickly made in the northern direction: toward Paris. Led by General Patton, a heavily armored force was soon just south of the capital. With resistance inside the city reaching a peak, General Eisenhower called for a direct assault.

On August 25, 1944, General Dietrich von Choltitz disobeyed Hitler's orders to destroy Paris from within and surrendered to the Allies. Now the German position in Europe was in decline, and the Allies were on a roll toward Berlin.

Soon after regaining France, the British liberated Brussels, and in October, the Americans crossed the German border and captured the town of Aachen. But the resistance to the advance was not over. The Germans were now fighting for their very existence. When 10,000 British troops were dropped behind the lines in the Netherlands, the Germans captured or killed almost three-quarters of the advancing army, and the Allied push stalled.

On December 16, 1944, in a desperate attempt to regain lost ground, the Germans struck in a surprise attack against the Allies in the Ardennes. Supported by hundreds of tanks, 550,000 German troops initially took a lot of ground in what is known as the Battle of the Bulge.

"We passed through Malmedy, then entered the woods to replace units in the 9th Division," recalled Carmen Capalbo, an eighteen-year-old draftee. His division marched into the Ardennes Forest to replace a veteran unit:

> Our outfit was walking up one side of a road and they were coming down the other side. I'll never forget the visual difference. There was something in their eyes I can't describe. Some people talk of the 1,000 yard stare. What I saw was

the look of combat. These guys were the same age as we were but they seemed 100 years older. I realized then that we were facing something different.[6]

This was indeed an unusually ferocious battle, where hand-to-hand combat and confusion were commonplace. The fighting lasted for weeks in the snow-covered woods. Charles MacDonald, the commander of Company I, summed up the desperate fighting that took place on the second day of the battle when

> wave after wave of fanatically screaming German infantry stormed the slight tree-covered rise held by the three platoons. A continuous hail of fire exuded from their weapons, answered by volley after volley from the defenders. Germans fell right and left. The few rounds of artillery we did succeed in bringing down caught the attackers in the draw to our front, and we could hear their screams of pain when the small-arms fire would slacken. But still they came![7]

In a desperate attempt to save his troops from the never-ending infantry assault and the artillery fire from tanks moving into position, Captain MacDonald ordered his men to take positions farther to the rear. Two soldiers (who later received the Medal of Honor) covered the retreat by pouring small-arms fire into the advancing Germans. Nothing could stop them, however, and soon all of the company was dodging bullets and running for safety.

Not long afterward, the bad weather that had grounded American aircraft at the beginning of the great battle cleared. Once the planes could hit back at the advancing Germans, the tide was turned. The German counteroffensive failed, and the Allied advance into German territory continued once more.

As commander of the Third Army in 1944, General George Patton led his troops in an amazing series of swift advances across France. By the time Germany surrendered, Patton's army held much of what became the American occupation zone.

THE END IN EUROPE

With the Russians pushing from the east and the Allies moving in from the west, the Germans surrendered town after town. Allied forces began to free the prisoners who had survived the ghastly concentration camps. For the first time, many Americans and others around the world began to realize what terrible crimes the Nazis had committed against humanity, crimes that shall never be forgotten. Hitler's plan to make his world free of Jews and others he considered undesirable shocked and appalled Allied soldiers who were there to liberate the death camps.

Until the United States declared war on Germany and joined the Allies, there seemed to be a concerted effort to ignore the stories that came from Europe of brutalities. Hitler's policy of imprisoning and killing German, Polish, and Slavic Jews, Gypsies, and others the dictator called "inferior" perhaps seemed to be some horrible fantasy tale to those Americans who heard about such atrocities. However, liberation of the camps and a great deal of evidence gathered after the war clearly showed that Hitler's government was responsible for the systematic murder of six million Jews and millions of other Europeans.

Nerin E. Gun, a former Berlin resident, was one of the few international journalists imprisoned in a concentration camp, and while a prisoner he spent time in one of the worst hellholes—Dachau in Germany. The camp was a converted munitions plant that was designed for 5,000 prisoners but was crammed with 35,000 at the time Gun was held. When American army troops liberated that camp, what they saw drove many of them "raving mad," as Gun put it. They were ready to destroy every Gestapo agent or member of the secret state police (SS) in sight.

American soldiers who advanced on the town of Dachau found cattle cars full of more than 2,000 corpses: Hungarian and Polish Jews, men, women, and children, who had been starved, suffocated, or beaten to death even before they got to the concentration camp itself. When the Americans reached the gates of the prison, "some of the SS men on the watchtowers started to shoot into the mobs of prisoners," Gun recalled in a book about his experiences. At that point, the

> Americans threw all caution to the winds. They opened fire on the towers. . . . Then the hunt started for any other Germans in SS uniforms. Within a quarter of an hour there was not a single one of the Hitler henchmen alive within the camp. . . . When there were no more SS men to go after, the GIs machine-gunned the dogs which were kept in the camp's huge kennel.
>
> Then came . . . those who had just been saved, the mass of scarred, pate-shaven ones with their haggard, livid faces, their smiles grotesque because of their broken teeth,

these human wrecks who embraced you, threw themselves on you, tried to tell you their stories in sign language, led you by the hand to show you the hovels they lived in, the dead outside the barracks, the dying in the hospital. The Americans gave them cigarettes, their rations, their chewing gum, their addresses, even the jackets or overcoats off their backs, or simply emptied their pockets to them.[8]

Prisoners at Dachau concentration camp cheered their liberators, the 42nd Rainbow Division of the U.S. Army.

On April 30, 1945, General Eisenhower dictated a terse message to the U.S. president and the Allied command: "Our forces liberated and mopped up the infamous concentration camp at Dachau. Approximately 32,000 prisoners were liberated. Three hundred SS camp guards were quickly neutralized."[9] That same day, Adolf Hitler committed suicide in Berlin. A week later, on May 7, the German army surrendered. The war in Europe was finally at an end.

Six

JAPAN AND THE BOMB

*B*efore the United States and the other Allies turned their attention from the war in Europe to concentrate on ending the battles in the Pacific, a young navy lieutenant who would later become president of the United States was in the Solomon Islands. He was John F. Kennedy, one of the many thousands of Americans taking part in the island-hopping strategy that was intended to stop Japanese aggression. The plan was to invade each island, control it, then move on to the next. In the process, many men were lost, and Kennedy himself barely escaped death when his boat, the PT 109, was sunk during a battle. Some of his crew were not so lucky, as he explained to his parents in a letter written in 1943:

> One had ridden with me for as long as I had been out here. He had been somewhat shocked by a bomb that had landed near the boat about two weeks before. He never really got over it; he always seemed to have the feeling that something was going to happen to him....When a fellow gets the feeling that he's in for it, the only thing to do is to let him get off the boat because strangely enough, they always seem to be the ones that do get it.

Kennedy noted that the death of crew members "certainly brought home how real the war is," and went on to complain about the "experts" who would write in the home papers about the need to "fight the Japs for years if necessary . . . sacrifice hundreds of thousands. . . . People get so used to talking about billions of dollars and millions of soldiers that thousands of dead sounds like drops in the bucket." Then Kennedy ended his letter with a prophetic statement: "Perhaps all of that won't be necessary—and it can all be done by bombing."[1]

For a while, incredible heroic efforts on the part of many Allied soldiers, sailors, and marines continued, and many lives and dollars were eventually sacrificed in the campaign to liberate the territory that had been captured by the Japanese. But the end was finally achieved with bombs.

JAPANESE FEEL THE PAIN

Fumiko Nakane was only sixteen years old, working as a nurse on the island of Okinawa, Japan, in June of 1945 when she and her family experienced just a taste of the devastation that was dropped from the sky. She described one particularly grizzly incident that occurred when the bombs and shells flew:

> Naval gunfire from the American ships off the coast intensified and took the life of my elder sister—among countless others. According to the story I heard later from her mother-in-law, my sister had been nursing her infant child under a tree. Suddenly the baby screamed. My sister's mother-in-law turned quickly to see my sister, headless but still holding to her breast her infant, now bathed in blood gushing from the stump of the mother's neck. My sister was buried without a head.
>
> Many people were buried in the very craters where American naval bombardments had killed them, only to be exhumed when other shells landed in the same place. Soon there was nowhere to lay the dead.[2]

A U.S. battleship shells Okinawa as troops invade the island.

ON THE RUN

Japan was under considerable pressure now. Naval and air defeats were commonplace, and the loss of equipment and lives was horrendous. Three million Japanese troops were still deployed throughout the Pacific and China, but the government was no longer capable of supplying them. The Allied advance ground on as the Philippines, Burma, Iwo Jima, and Okinawa were subdued in fierce and costly campaigns.

Instrumental to these successes was the ability of commanders to communicate their plans without having them discovered by the enemy. All participants in the war used radio communication to set positions, give orders, call in air strikes, and so on, and all used elaborate secret codes to protect their messages. Each side employed code breakers to decipher the enemy's transmissions whenever they could. Often a new code was broken in a matter of days or even hours, shifting the advantage from those who sent the code to those who had broken it.

U.S. forces were able to communicate secretly with the help of 420 code talkers, who were assigned to many marine units fighting in the Pacific theater. The code talkers were members of the Navajo nation, Native Americans who fought with pride and distinction throughout the war. They helped develop a code that was based on the Navajo tongue—a spoken language that was totally indecipherable to the Japanese.

The code talkers were especially helpful during the battle for Iwo Jima, a monthlong slaughter in which three of their number were killed. Six networks were established there to send over 800 messages during the fighting. As Major Howard Conner said, "Without the Navajos the Marines would never have taken Iwo Jima."[3]

THE HORRIBLE END

By July 1945, Allied bombs had destroyed half of Tokyo and many other towns and cities. An invasion of Japan was imminent, but a separate development halted those plans.

Navajo code talkers were among the first Marines to hit the beach on Saipan.

A group of scientists had just completed years of work on a highly secret program called the Manhattan Project, to develop an atomic bomb. The bomb was successfully tested at Alamogordo, New Mexico, on July 16. President Harry S. Truman, now in the Oval Office after the death of Franklin Roosevelt, made the decision to drop this powerful bomb on Japan. He believed such an action would actually save lives, as compared to a full invasion of the country.

On July 26, 1945, Truman, Churchill, and the Chinese leader Chiang Kai-shek told Japan to surrender or face devastation. The new bomb was not mentioned, and the Japanese ignored the ultimatum. On August 6, a single American bomber, a B-29 Superfortress dubbed the *Enola Gay*, dropped the first nuclear device ever used against humans on Hiroshima, Japan. Within seconds, 75 percent of the city was vaporized.

Sumiko Kirihara was fourteen and living in Hiroshima at that time. On that fateful day, she and others were actually "relieved to hear the sound of only one airplane flying over the city." She recalled what happened next:

Suddenly a tremendous cracking sound nearly split my eardrums. A pale blue flash temporarily blinded me; then total darkness enveloped everything. When the light once again penetrated the blackness, I saw the city of Hiroshima reduced to ruins. In a vast area of flattened buildings, I could find only three standing . . . and our own two-story wooden house, by some miracle almost undamaged. Among the fallen timbers and over the shattered glass in the streets, people wandered to and fro.

Fire now raged everywhere. A black rain fell . . . smoke hid the sun. As we made our way to the Kyobashi River, whirlwinds tossed sheets of scorched galvanized iron along the streets. Then the winds struck the river, sending columns of water upward, dashing boats about, and heading directly for the place where we were standing. In terror, I dug a hole in the sand, crawled into it, and held my clothing to my body for fear it would be blown away. One whirlwind followed another raising clouds of sand that lashed at my back like countless needles. Unable to bear the winds any longer, we climbed to a piece of open land by the river. But the heat was so great that we were forced to enter the water.[4]

The Kyobashi River (left) is filled with debris after the A-bomb was dropped on Hiroshima on August 6, 1945. Most of the city—about five square miles—was destroyed.

After the blast, another resident, Mitsuko Hatano, tried to find a sister who had not returned to the family home located miles from the city. Accompanied by a neighbor who was also searching for someone, Mitsuko "wandered aimlessly," unsure where to go. She reported:

I searched everywhere for my sister. I went to the place where her apartment had stood and to the location where her office had once been ... at the hypocenter of the explosion.

A layer of white ash covered the ruins that were all that remained. Soldiers were attempting to haul away the corpses buried in heaps of broken tiles, shattered glass, and charred wood. But the dead were too numerous for the living to attend to. Days of searching produced no signs of my sister. Since it seemed improbable that she could have survived, I collected a few still-warm bones from the ground, wrapped them in cloth, and took them home to my waiting parents.[5]

The effects of the nuclear bomb eventually killed 75,000 people. A second bomb was dropped on another city, Nagasaki, three days after the Hiroshima blast, and the Japanese military command finally asked for peace.

The Japanese signed the surrender aboard the U.S. battleship Missouri *on September 2, 1945. General of the Army Douglas MacArthur (far right) signed for the Allies.*

Barrie Greenbie, who was serving with U.S. forces in the Philippines, tried to make some sense out of all the devastation and death. He wrote to his wife on August 9 that it was

> like getting a first hand look at hell or a preview of the end of the world. Looks like this will have to be the last war for freedom because after the next there won't be any world left to be free. Maybe it's a good thing. Maybe even the most degenerate tyrants will hesitate to commit world suicide . . . or perhaps the people of the world will be so scared that they will never put their fingers near the fuse of such power.[6]

Source Notes

One

1. Thurston Clarke, *Pearl Harbor Ghosts* (New York: William Morrow and Company, 1991), 157.

2. Quoted in Annette Tapert, ed., *Lines of Battle: Letters from American Servicemen, 1941–1945* (New York: Times Books, 1987), 8.

3. Quoted in Studs Terkel, *"The Good War": An Oral History of World War Two* (New York: Pantheon Books, 1984), 19.

4. Ibid., 34.

5. Response from Horace Basham posted in "Project Memories for Children in Project Chatback," electronic listserv, March 25, 1994.

Two

1. Alice-Leone Moats, *A Blind Date with Mars* (Garden City, N.Y.: Doubleday, Doran and Company, 1943), quoted in Harold Elk Straubing, ed., *A Taste of War: Eyewitness Accounts of World War II* (New York: Sterling, 1992), 266–267.

2. Quoted in Paul Fridlund, "The Will to Live (World War II Diary)," *American History*, September/October 1993, 51.

3. Quoted in Tapert, *Lines of Battle*, 20–22.

4. Robert L. Scott, *God Is My Co-Pilot* (New York: Ballantine Books, 1943), 132.

5. Quoted in John M. Blum et al., *The National Experience*, Part 2, 2d ed. (New York: Harcourt, Brace and World, 1968), 735.

Three

1. Kiyo Sato Viacrucis, "A Teenage Diary from an American Concentration Camp" (article for a creative writing class, 1972, and interview by Kathlyn Gay, Elkhart, Indiana, 1972).

2. Quoted in Mary Pat Beal, "Former WAVE Salutes Their Role in World War II," *South Bend Tribune*, January 15, 1995, F9.

3. Quoted in Marianne Verges, *On Silver Wings: The Women Airforce Service Pilots of World War II 1942–1944* (New York: Ballantine Books, 1991), 46.

4. Nell Giles, *Punch In, Susie!: A Woman's War Factory Diary* (New York: Harper and Brothers, 1943), 1.

5. Response from Anne Oliver posted in "Project Memories for Children in Project Chatback," electronic listserv, February 20, 1994.

6. "How to Use the War Ration Book," OPA Form No. R-303 (Washington, D.C.: U.S. Government Printing Office, 1943).

Four

1. Giles, *Punch In, Susie!*, 78.

2. Siegfried Knappe with Ted Brusaw, *Soldat: Reflections of a German Soldier, 1936–1949* (New York: Dell, 1992), 222–223.

3. Response from Walter Felscher posted in "Project Memories for Children in Project Chatback," electronic listserv, February 21, 1994.

Five

1. Basham in "Project Memories."

2. Quoted in Tapert, *Lines of Battle*, 161.

3. Quoted in Peter M. Bergman, *The Chronological*

History of the Negro in America (New York: Harper & Row, 1969), 503.

4. Robert W. Mullen, *Blacks in America's Wars* (New York: Pathfinder, 1991), 55.

5. Cynthia Tucker, "Black Vets Fought Two Wars," *Seattle Times,* June 6, 1994, B6.

6. Quoted in Gerald Astor, *A Blood-Dimmed Tide: The Battle of the Bulge by the Men Who Fought It* (New York: Dell, 1992), 24.

7. Ibid., 134–135.

8. Nerin E. Gun, *The Day of the Americans* (New York: Fleet Publishing Corporation, 1966), quoted in Straubing, *A Taste of War*, 255–256.

9. Ibid., 257.

Six

1. Quoted in Tapert, *Lines of Battle*, 117.

2. Quoted in Youth Division of Soka Gakkai, *Cries For Peace: Experiences of Japanese Victims of World War II* (Tokyo: Japan Times, 1978), 38.

3. Quoted in Bruce Watson, "Jaysho, moasi, dibeh, ayeshi, hasclishnih, beshlo, shush, gini," *Smithsonian*, August 1993, 40.

4. Quoted in Soka Gakkai, *Cries For Peace*, 178–179.

5. Ibid., 177.

6. Quoted in Tapert, *Lines of Battle*, 286–287.

Further Reading

Aaseng, Nathan. *Paris*. New York: New Discovery, 1992.

Ayer, Eleanor. *Berlin*. New York: New Discovery, 1992.

Bliven, Bruce, Jr. *The Story of D-Day: June 6, 1944*. New York: Random House, 1994.

Frank, Anne. *Anne Frank: The Diary of a Young Girl*. Introduction by Eleanor Roosevelt. New York: Doubleday, 1967.

Hanmer, Trudy J. *Leningrad*. New York: New Discovery, 1992.

Kronenwetter, Michael. *London*. New York: New Discovery, 1992.

Nardo, Don. *World War Two: The War in the Pacific*. San Diego: Lucent, 1991.

Newton, Robert. *Tokyo*. New York: New Discovery, 1992.

Pfeifer, Kathryn B. *The 761st Tank Battalion*. New York: Twenty-First Century Books, 1994.

Sherrow, Victoria. *Amsterdam*. New York: New Discovery, 1992.

Stein, Conrad R. *World War II in the Pacific: "Remember Pearl Harbor."* Hillside, N.J.: Enslow, 1994.

Toll, Nelly. *Behind the Secret Window: A Memoir of a Hidden Childhood*. New York: Dial, 1993.

Westerfield, Scott. *The Berlin Airlift*. Morristown, N.J.: Silver Burdett, 1989.

Index